art for all seasons

Marilyn Barnes

Acknowledgements

Piece It Together (page 19)

I wish to thank the staff and children at Nicholas Hawksmoor Primary School. Special thanks go to head teacher Richard Edwards for being a truly wonderful supporter of the arts. Special thanks to all the children who attend my art club and to all those who have contributed to the work in this book. Two very talented students from Goldsmiths College, London, deserve a thank you for augmenting the Outdoor World display, namely Catherine Rock and Dee Maguire. This large hanging was on display in the Tate Modern in London in 2001.

First published in 2002 by BELAIR PUBLICATIONS LIMITED
Apex Business Centre, Boscombe Road, Dunstable, Bedfordshire, LU5 4RL.

© 2002 Folens on behalf of the author Marilyn Barnes

Commissioning Editor: Karen McCaffery
Design: Jane Conway
Illustrator: Jane Conway (seasonal text boxes, icons and diagrams on page 33)

Editor: Elizabeth Miles
Cover design: Ed Gallagher
Photography: Kelvin Freeman

ISBN 0 94788 292 8

The cover photograph is taken from page 63 (3D Ice-cream Pictures).

Contents

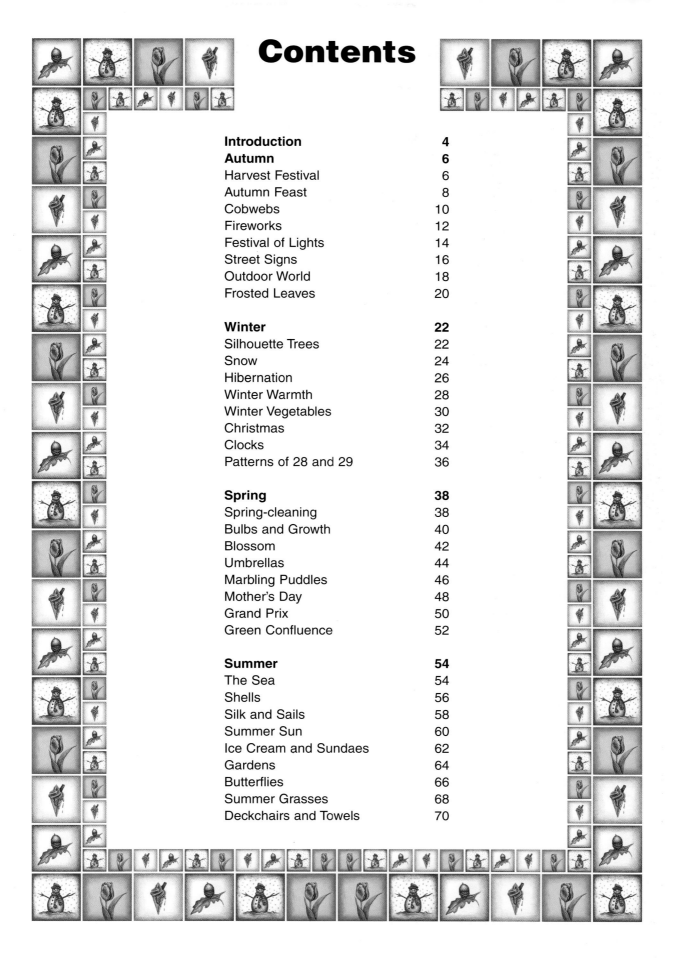

Introduction

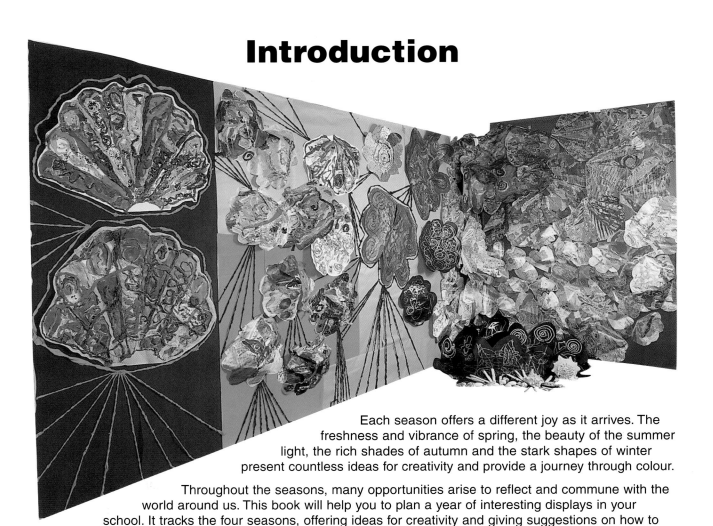

Each season offers a different joy as it arrives. The freshness and vibrance of spring, the beauty of the summer light, the rich shades of autumn and the stark shapes of winter present countless ideas for creativity and provide a journey through colour.

Throughout the seasons, many opportunities arise to reflect and commune with the world around us. This book will help you to plan a year of interesting displays in your school. It tracks the four seasons, offering ideas for creativity and giving suggestions on how to display the children's work in dynamic ways. The ideas are intended as starting points that will launch you with confidence into producing new displays, of which you can be proud.

The atmosphere created through display can enhance children's learning. A calm ambience can be created with soft lighting from lamps, and can encourage an awareness of the light and shade that surround us in the natural world. Plants can also bring life into displays.

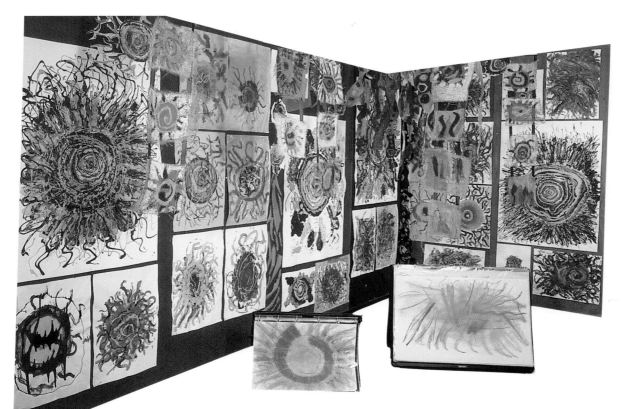

Artefacts, choice of backing papers, edging rolls, interesting fabrics and display units can all take display in different directions. If possible, try to collect display materials with many shades of one colour. This will help enliven your work throughout the seasons. Specialist lighting will also help to illuminate the quality of effort offered by the children and bring professionalism to their work.

It is a good idea to collect objects that stimulate the minds of young children, if only to encourage comment, elicit feelings or celebrate a similarity between themselves and something already produced. Sculptures, prints or paintings can be purchased for use as stimuli and to add character to the school.

Good display can make the difference between existing and living. It will educate the feelings and increase sensitivity. Which of us in our own homes would be thrilled by blank walls, bright garish lighting and a poor quality finish? Some children we teach spend more time in school than they do with their parents who brought them into the world. Have we not a duty each year to create a challenging, changing, questioning environment, which will stimulate heart, mind and body and lead to success?

Whether we are working from first-hand experience or from imagination, the skill of the teacher to display work in a sensitive or dynamic way will have a moving effect on all who see it.

Harvest Festival

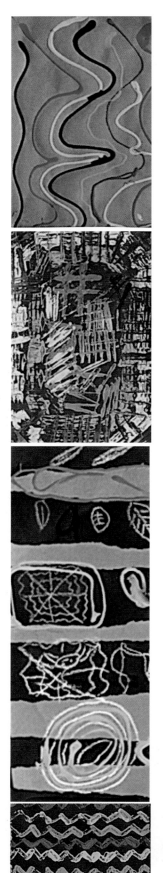

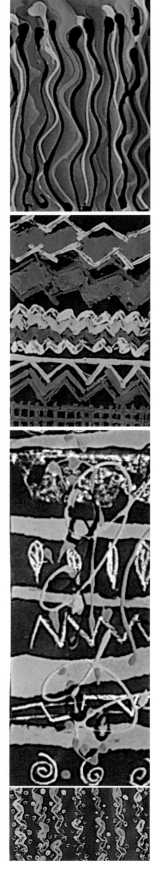

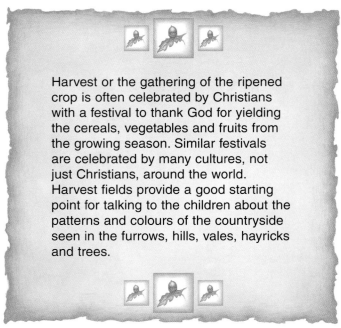

Harvest or the gathering of the ripened crop is often celebrated by Christians with a festival to thank God for yielding the cereals, vegetables and fruits from the growing season. Similar festivals are celebrated by many cultures, not just Christians, around the world. Harvest fields provide a good starting point for talking to the children about the patterns and colours of the countryside seen in the furrows, hills, vales, hayricks and trees.

Harvest Prints and Collages

Materials

Paper (black, brown, green)
Poster paint (yellow, black, brown, green)
New Plasticine strips
Chalk
Paintbrushes
PVA glue

Methods

a. Use bottles of yellow, black, brown and green poster paints to pour crop-and-furrow patterns onto brown paper.
b. Create crop patterns on black paper using paintbrushes or by printing with new Plasticine strips which are already formed in lines.
c. Glue ripped lines of green paper down the page and decorate between the lines with chalk patterns. Pour yellow, black or green patterns of paint over the collage.

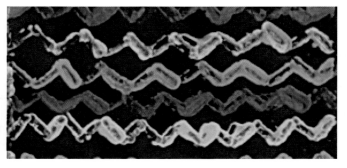

Harvest Fields Landscape

Materials

Black paper ripped into furrow
    shapes
New Plasticine strips
Poster paint (yellow, black,
    brown, green)
Art straws
Gold crêpe paper
Green paper strips
Paintbrushes
Mixing palettes
Water pots
PVA glue

Method

1. Randomly print crop patterns
   on black paper, using new
   Plasticine strips which
   are formed in lines.
2. When the paper is covered,
   pattern further by creating
   a collage with either gold or
   green paper strips or art
   straws, following the ripped
   edge.
3. Piece together each strip of
   black paper to create a large
   harvest landscape display.
4. Finally, pour paint spirals
   straight from the bottle all over
   the artwork.

Display

1. Display children's harvest
   prints and collage pictures
   individually in vertical lines
   down the wall. Add strips of
   ripped paper between pictures
   in harvest colours to create an
   undulating landscape of
   furrows, hills and vales.
2. Overlap long strips of printing
   and collage work to create a
   rich fuller image of the
   harvest landscape for a
   special large scale harvest
   montage.
3. Intersperse large scale
   display work with individual
   harvest prints and collages.

Autumn Feast

Autumn Pictures

Materials

White paper (2 sizes)
Cellophane (yellow, orange, red, green)
PVA glue
Acrylic paint (yellow, orange, red, green)

Ripped paper (orange, red, green)
Pastels
Wax crayons
Chalks

Method

1. Create a ripped paper collage on white backing paper. Draw autumnal objects, for example leaves, cobwebs and conkers.
2. Rip Cellophane and coloured paper into strips and glue them on top of the drawings.
3. Finish by pouring acrylic paint straight from the bottle to form large autumn leaves. Remember to add details such as veins and stalks.

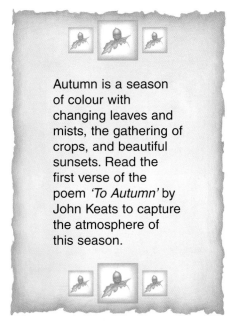

Autumn is a season of colour with changing leaves and mists, the gathering of crops, and beautiful sunsets. Read the first verse of the poem *'To Autumn'* by John Keats to capture the atmosphere of this season.

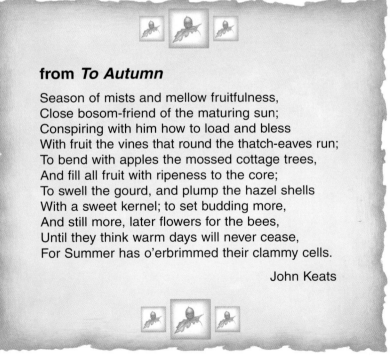

from *To Autumn*

Season of mists and mellow fruitfulness,
Close bosom-friend of the maturing sun;
Conspiring with him how to load and bless
With fruit the vines that round the thatch-eaves run;
To bend with apples the mossed cottage trees,
And fill all fruit with ripeness to the core;
To swell the gourd, and plump the hazel shells
With a sweet kernel; to set budding more,
And still more, later flowers for the bees,
Until they think warm days will never cease,
For Summer has o'erbrimmed their clammy cells.

John Keats

Display

1. Cover the walls with autumn-coloured backing paper.
2. Sort the art work into different sized sheets and place the largest work around the wall, one above the other.
3. Staple ripped Cellophane strips around the work so that the strips are free to move.
4. Arrange the smaller pictures in vertical lines between the largest work.
5. Use gold edging to enhance chosen pictures and repeat the Cellophane where space allows.
6. Hang lengths of gold chain between the work to catch the light.

Cobwebs

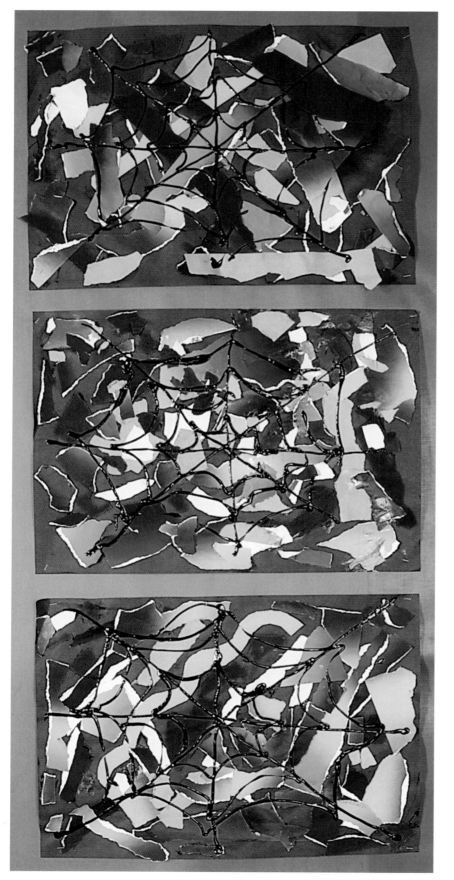

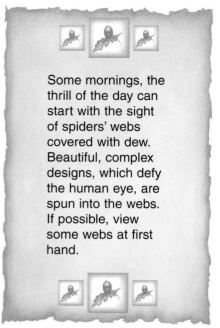

Some mornings, the thrill of the day can start with the sight of spiders' webs covered with dew. Beautiful, complex designs, which defy the human eye, are spun into the webs. If possible, view some webs at first hand.

Web Collage

Materials

Black paper
Rainbow paper
Coloured paper (red, yellow, green, blue, orange)
Black acrylic paint
PVA glue

Method

1. Cover black paper with a large circular collage of torn coloured paper.
2. Keep making circles smaller and smaller until there are about six or seven. One of the circles can be torn from the rainbow paper.
3. Collage the circles, slightly overlapping in decreasing sizes.
4. Make a poured-paint cobweb over the top of the picture, but first practise drawing a cobweb on paper.
5. Remind the children that there are threads that support the web. The spider wraps the thread around the supports in a loose pattern.

Sand Webs

Materials

Black paper   Coloured sands
PVA glue   Drawing pencils

Method

1. Draw a large web in pencil on black paper.
2. Cover the web with PVA glue (a section at a time), then cover it with coloured sand.
3. Keep gluing portions of the web until it is all covered with sand.
4. Allow the webs to dry.

Display

1. Cover the walls with green and orange backing paper. Alternate the two types of picture in vertical rows.
2. Display web pictures on a complementary coloured backing and block together.
3. Use black paper edging roll to make a huge spider's web over the top of the display.

Fireworks

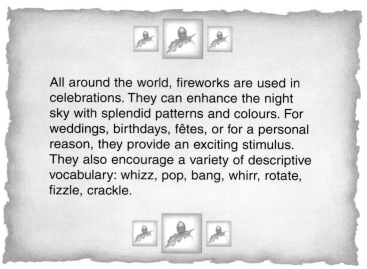

All around the world, fireworks are used in celebrations. They can enhance the night sky with splendid patterns and colours. For weddings, birthdays, fêtes, or for a personal reason, they provide an exciting stimulus. They also encourage a variety of descriptive vocabulary: whizz, pop, bang, whirr, rotate, fizzle, crackle.

Firework Collage

Materials

Blue sugar paper
Art straws
Fluorescent paint (red,
    blue, pink, green, yellow)
Paintbrushes

Water pots
Silver strips of paper/foil
Foil, cut into squares
PVA glue

Note: Fluorescent paint will not mix. (Mixing results in a dull brown colour.)

Method

1. Cover art straws with fluorescent paints.
2. When dry, use them to make firework patterns (spirals, dots, zigzags) and glue them onto sheets of blue sugar paper to make a collage.
3. Add patterns of silver foil to the collage.
4. Add showers of foil squares to form spirals or zigzags.

Pointillist Fireworks

Materials

Black paper
Fluorescent paint (red, blue, pink, green, yellow)
Small paintbrushes
Water

Method

1. Work in groups of three or four children. Give each group a large sheet of black paper.
2. Demonstrate the pointillist technique of painting with the brush at right angles to the paper.
3. Paint exploding pointillist fireworks using, for example, spirals, lines, zigzags and shower shapes.
4. Fill the background with further dots in lines or patterns. The fuller the pattern becomes, the better.

Display

1. Since much of the work is produced on black paper, it is a good idea to use brightly coloured backing paper in the display. Greens and blues in particular will enhance the effect.
2. Display the artwork in vertical lines down the walls, or diagonally at angles to one another.
3. Use lengths of green foil to add zigzag firework patterns between the works.
4. Cut strips of foil into half-metre lengths and create exploding fireworks over the art by stapling the ends onto the wall and allowing the foil to fall forwards.

Festival of Lights

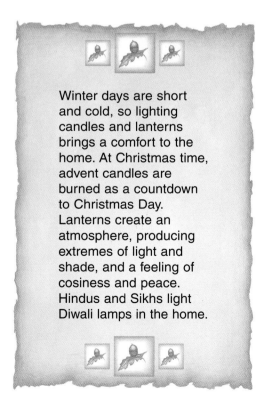

Pastel Patterns

Materials

Collection of candles, lanterns
Black paper
Pastels (grey, black, white, red, yellow, orange, green)
Selection of coloured glitter
PVA glue

Method

1. Arrange the candlesticks and lanterns into a display with all the items lit. Use the display to discuss light and shade. Ask the children:

   – How does the light affect colour?
   – Does the light change the background?
   – Does it create movement in the scene? If so, why?

2. Draw the candles and lanterns using pastels. Scale up the lanterns and look at the flames and the effects they create.
3. Smudge the pastels to gain warm effects.
4. Highlight selected areas by spreading glue and adding coloured glitter.

Winter days are short and cold, so lighting candles and lanterns brings a comfort to the home. At Christmas time, advent candles are burned as a countdown to Christmas Day. Lanterns create an atmosphere, producing extremes of light and shade, and a feeling of cosiness and peace. Hindus and Sikhs light Diwali lamps in the home.

Painted Lanterns

Materials

Set of glass paints   Gutta, silver or gold   Night lights

Method

1. Ask the children to bring in any old lanterns from home even if they are rusty. It is also possible to buy a variety of cheap lanterns.
2. If the lantern has removable glass sides, take them out to draw on the design. Draw the design in gutta and allow it to dry overnight. (The gutta needs a pin-prick to start it running.)
3. Paint the lanterns, keeping to a tight range of colours. Interesting effects can be gained by running the paint down the lantern.
4. When the paint is dry, place a night light in each lantern.

Display

1. Combine the pastel lantern wall display with a 3D-painted-lanterns display on a table top.
2. Place white backing paper on the wall and arrange the artwork with vertical lines running through the display.
3. Edge some of the work in silver or gold corrugated paper to add light to the display.
4. Place blocks or boxes on a table top to form the 3D display. Place the highest block in the middle, at the back. Cover the blocks with fabric and place the painted lanterns in strategic positions.
5. Add gold tinsel for more shine if desired.

Street Signs

Road markings and signs fill the busy streets, alerting us to possible hazards and danger. By highlighting these signs and markings, children will be reminded to cross the road in a safe place, such as controlled crossings, and drivers will be reminded to pay attention to speed limits and hazard warnings.

Materials

White cartridge paper
Drawing pencils
Acrylic paint (red, black, white, yellow, blue)
Paintbrushes
Mixing palettes
Water pots

Method

1. Observe road signs and make pencil sketches of them. Illustrate the variety of shapes and designs on offer.
2. When the page is full, fill in the background with patterns from road markings, traffic lights or similar items seen in the street.
3. Paint the picture with acrylic paint, being very careful with all the straight edges.
4. Fill in the background with similar colour choices to the items illustrated.

3D Road Signs

Materials

Cardboard
Drawing pencils
Scissors
Rulers

Acrylic paint (red, black, white, blue, yellow)
Compass
Water pots

Method

1. Draw large road signs on cardboard.
2. Cut out each one and paint it in the appropriate colours using acrylic paint.
3. Try to keep clear edges.

Display

1. Cover a display board with red backing paper. Liven it up by adding white road markings.
2. Staple each painting into place and edge with black edging roll, to create definite lines.
3. Use the edging roll to form triangles and road markings, speed limits or instructions found on roads.
4. Suspend 3D road signs from the ceiling in front of the display.

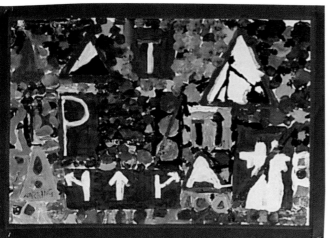

Outdoor World

The outdoor world offers acute experiences of colour, with extreme variations in light and shade. All the senses are stimulated and, by developing the themes of water, sky, nature and urban life, the imagination and creativity of the children will be enhanced.

Prepare stimulus boards for the themes: water, sky, nature or urban. Each board should include a collection of photographs, postcards and artwork linked to the theme.

Outdoor World – Water, Sky, Nature or Urban Life

Method

1. Organise the children into study groups for each theme and ask them to choose fabrics, colours and objects that suggest their subject.
2. Buy cheap wooden frames to mount individual studies of their water, sky, nature or urban theme.
3. Encourage a minimalist approach in representing their aspect of the world, using one idea to fill one small frame.
4. Paint, draw or make a collage in the frame. For example, the sea might be represented with shells, water might be rows of different shades of blue, nature might simply be an autumn leaf and an urban theme might be an old tin can stuck into the frame.

Piece It Together

Materials

4-metre wide roll of paper
Metre rulers
Pencils, scissors
Acrylic paint (primary colours:
  red, yellow, blue)
Fluorescent paint (pink, yellow,
  blue, orange, green)
Paintbrushes
Mixing palettes
Water pots
Pastels, oil pastels, crayons
Coloured sand
Cellophane (various colours)
Crêpe paper (various colours)
Art straws
Marbling inks
Items such as shells, bottle-tops,
  plastic bottles, mirrors, boxes
PVA glue

Method

1. Roll out the paper and draw angled shapes all over it, like a giant jigsaw.
2. Cut the lines to create up to 40 different shaped pieces.
3. Before separating the pieces, number them in two directions like a grid so that they can be easily reassembled.
4. Create a picture on each of the shaped pieces to represent the water, nature, sky or urban theme.
5. Encourage a variety of techniques, including pouring paint, flailing paint, painting with brushes and daubing with fabric. Try grating pastels over the paint for a different effect.
6. Encourage 3D features using, for example, scrunched-up paper or a variety of boxes.
7. Experiment with printing, mixing the media, ripping paper and marbling patterns.

Display

1. When the work is complete back each piece on card. Reassemble it to form a huge artwork and mount the whole artwork on large pieces of cardboard. Alternatively, it can be sewn together, laced with twine or string, or glued onto a huge roll of paper. Hang it up and leave to dry.

Frosted Leaves

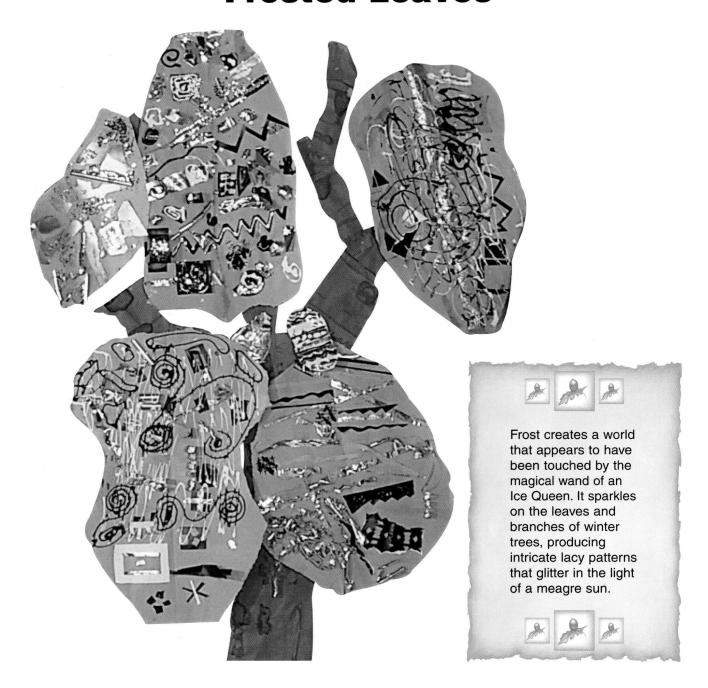

Frost creates a world that appears to have been touched by the magical wand of an Ice Queen. It sparkles on the leaves and branches of winter trees, producing intricate lacy patterns that glitter in the light of a meagre sun.

Frosted Collage Leaves

Materials

Cardboard cut into large leaf shapes
Gold and silver paper
Gold and silver ribbons
Paper for collage work

PVA glue
Acrylic paint (brown, black, white)
Art straws

Method

1. Design a frosted pattern on a large cardboard leaf. Use silver, gold and black paper, and ribbon to create the collage. Tear, curl, spiral, zigzag and pattern the leaf until it is full.
2. Finally, pour acrylic paint over the surface of the leaf in spirals, lines and veined patterns.

Collage Leaves

Materials

Cardboard leaves
Black paper for tearing
Spray paint (silver and gold)
Art straws
Glitter
PVA glue

Methods

a. Create 3D patterns on large cardboard leaves with pieces of ripped paper. Spray over them with silver or gold spray paint.
b. Use art straws sprayed silver or gold to create a veined leaf pattern. Areas of glue can be added to the leaf and glitter sprinkled over them.
c. Fill a tray with glitter, rip a small leaf shape from paper, cover it with glue and rub it on the glitter.

Display

1. Form the trunks of trees using twisted brown paper. Extend the trunk in places to form branches.
2. Staple the frosted collage leaves onto the tree, overlapping them until the tree is full.
3. Choose a variety of leaves for the tree as this will add pattern and texture.
4. Display all the remaining leaf variations by overlapping them to make a large frosted wall montage.

November Night

Listen...
With faint dry sound,
Like steps of passing ghosts,
The leaves, frost-crisped,
    break from the trees
And fall.

Adelaide Crapsey

Silhouette Trees

Winter can be a harsh landscape as many trees are devoid of leaves. They form stark patterns against a winter skyline and offer a good stimulus for art. Any art in black, white and grey can offer dynamic results as they present total light and absence of light. The trees are like skeletal forms against the harsh background of winter. It is the kind of weather that stings the skin but invigorates at the same time.

Winter Trees

Materials

3 large sheets of paper stuck together lengthways (natural grey/stone colours)
Newspaper
Tissue paper (black and white)
Pencils or chalk
Acrylic paint (brown, white, black)
PVA glue

Method

1. Draw a large winter tree to fill the area of the paper.
2. Observe gnarled patterns that exist on the surface of tree trunks.
3. Rip up long lengths of newspaper and tissue paper, and twist them together firmly.
4. Glue these twisted shapes onto the tree to create the trunk and branches. Suggest that they glue the line first, then attach the twisted paper.

Variations

a. Draw the tree in the same way but fill it with acrylic paint patterns poured straight from the bottle.
b. Make a tree using ripped paper pieces in natural colours.

Display

1. Display the trees side by side. A variety of tree types will provide more interest.
2. Gather translucent paper into rosettes and staple between the trees. As the paper reaches halfway down the display, let it drop to fall like a fan, and staple.

Tissue Silhouette Trees

Materials

White paper	Fine paintbrushes
Drawing pencils	Tissue paper (light blue, black)
Black ink or black acrylic paint	PVA glue

Method

1. Draw a winter tree in pencil, then paint over it with black ink or acrylic paint and leave to dry.
2. Tear the light blue tissue paper into lengths and stick them across the page edge to edge, overlaying as you go.
3. Paint another tree on top of the tissue paper.
4. Use black tissue paper to form a 3D twisted tree pattern on top.
5. Finally cover the whole picture with a layer of light blue tissue paper.

Display

1. Cover the wall with blue backing paper and staple some of the pictures onto the background.
2. Tear around the edges of some of the pictures, following the outlines of the trees.
3. Hang additional pictures in front of the wall display by making two holes in the top of the paper and threading a silver length of foil through.

Snow

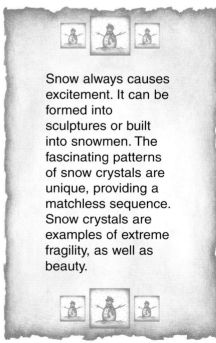

Snow always causes excitement. It can be formed into sculptures or built into snowmen. The fascinating patterns of snow crystals are unique, providing a matchless sequence. Snow crystals are examples of extreme fragility, as well as beauty.

3D Snow Crystals

Materials

Art straws	Paper doilies	Silver paper
PVA glue	Blue tissue paper	Stapler

Method

1. Cross over three art straws, held 60 degrees apart.
2. Either staple them or stick them together to form the crystal.
3. Discuss the symmetry in a crystal (each 'leg' has the same pattern).
4. Twist, curl and zigzag the straws to make different patterns. Explore all the different ways they can be used. For example, cut them open, stand them up straight and lay them flat.

Variation

Use art straws to form the crystal. Add patterns with doilies, tissue paper, zigzags of straws, or silver and blue foil, by adding them to the basic frame to create a collage effect.

Snowmen

Materials

White paper
Drawing pencils
Acrylic paint (white, blue)
Pearlised paint (red, blue, silver, gold, green, purple)

Paintbrushes
Mixing palettes
Water pots

Method

1. On paper, draw a large snowman on paper with interesting features, such as hat, eyes, mouth, pipe and scarf.
2. Paint the snowman with white acrylic paint as this will shine when dry.
3. Using a small paintbrush, paint all the details on the snowman in bright pearlised paints.
4. Fill the background with snowflake patterns or paint a very pale blue.

Display

1. Prepare a background with light blue backing paper.
2. Staple the snowmen onto the background, leaving spaces between them.
3. Take some black tissue paper and twist it to form a tree. Arch it out from the wall so that you can hang silver strands from it.
4. Twist lengths of silver foil paper to form icicles between the snowmen.
5. Hang the snow crystal designs in front of the display or staple them to the wall. Keep adding patterns until the scene looks full and vibrant.

Hibernation

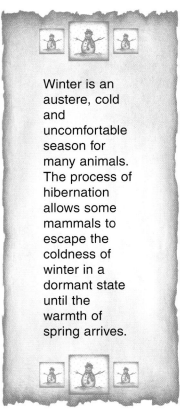

Winter is an austere, cold and uncomfortable season for many animals. The process of hibernation allows some mammals to escape the coldness of winter in a dormant state until the warmth of spring arrives.

Hibernating Animals – Hedgehog and Tortoise

Ask the children:

– Which animals hibernate?
– Why do they hibernate?
– What do the animals have to do before they go to sleep for the winter?

Materials

Small cardboard boxes	Paintbrushes	Tissue paper (green shades)	Art straws
White cartridge paper	Acrylic paint (brown)	Clear cellophane strips	PVA glue

Box

1. Paint the inside and outside of a small cardboard box brown.
2. Twist tissue paper in different shades of green and glue it inside the box to soften the home for the creature.
3. Hang strips of tissue paper, green foil or crêpe paper over the front of the box.

Hedgehog

1. Form a dome-shape by folding a sheet of paper underneath itself, tucking it in until the shape resembles a hedgehog. Paint it brown.
2. Cut art straws and stick them onto the body to form prickles.
3. Paint the prickles brown and add other details such as eyes and a nose.
4. Place the finished hedgehog inside the prepared box.

Tortoise

1. Form paper to make a dome-shape by tucking it underneath to create the shell of the tortoise.
2. Roll paper to form the head and the legs, and glue them into place under the shell.
3. Paint the tortoise in shades of green and brown, adding pattern details to its shell.
4. Place the finished tortoise inside the prepared box.

Hibernation Environment

Materials

Craft paper (brown)
Pastels (green, yellow)
Tissue paper (green shades)
Clear Cellophane strips
Acrylic paint (greens, yellows, browns)
Paintbrushes
Water pots
Brown hessian
Dried grasses

Method

1. Staple brown craft paper onto the wall.
2. Draw a natural environment on the paper, for example twigs and leaves.
3. Twist lengths of green tissue paper and hang from the ceiling.
4. Cut strips of Cellophane and paint leaves on them in acrylic paint. Hang them from the ceiling in front of the display.
5. Drape brown hessian around the display to create a natural-looking environment.
6. Continue to build the display, weaving dried grasses in and out.
7. Add further details in pastels and paint.

Winter Warmth

Painted Gloves

Discuss the need to wrap up warmly in winter. Ask the children:

– How do we keep warm?
– What about our hands and feet?
– What do you think are the best materials to keep us warm?

Materials

Choice of paper sizes	Paintbrushes
Thin charcoal	Mixing palettes
Acrylic paint (red, black, white)	Water pots

Method

1. Draw around your hand to form a mitten shape.
2. Draw around your hand again, now with the fingers spread apart, to form a glove shape.
3. Repeat the two ideas to form an interesting pattern and design.
4. Draw scarves between the hands if desired and add patterns to some of the items.
5. Fill in the background with grey, white, black and red acrylic paint. Only mix two colours (black and white). Keep the red and white clean.

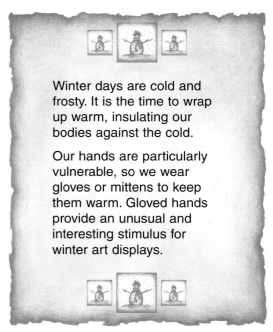

Winter days are cold and frosty. It is the time to wrap up warm, insulating our bodies against the cold.

Our hands are particularly vulnerable, so we wear gloves or mittens to keep them warm. Gloved hands provide an unusual and interesting stimulus for winter art displays.

Mitten Mobiles

Materials

Corrugated cardboard	Acrylic paint (red, black, white)	Water pots
Drawing pencils	Paintbrushes	Craft scissors

Method

1. Draw around your hand on corrugated cardboard to form glove and mitten shapes.
2. Cut out the shapes using craft scissors.
3. Add patterns to the cardboard gloves and mittens.
4. Cover both sides with acrylic paint.
5. Suspend the shapes from the ceiling to create a mitten mobile.

Display

1. Place black backing paper diagonally across a display board.
2. Fill the spaces with white paper.
3. Display the work, following the line of the black paper.
4. Paint polystyrene tiles red, black or white and attach to the wall. Use as a mount for a cut-out cardboard mitten or glove.
5. Hang the mitten mobiles from string or twisted tissue paper and suspend from the polystyrene tiles or the ceiling.

Winter Vegetables

Red Onions

Materials

Knives, chopping boards
Red onions
White paper
Drawing pencils
Ready-mixed paint (blue, red, white) and oil pastels
Paintbrushes
Mixing palettes
Water pots

Method

1. Prepare the onions, slicing them into rings, and closely observe the patterns. They can be complicated and extremely pretty.
2. Using a pencil, draw the patterns of the onions.
3. Colour-mix the closest shades of purple possible and paint the patterns.

Variations

a. Pour red, blue and white paint stripes straight from the bottle, then print with half an onion in straight rows.
b. Use oil pastels in blue and red to draw alternate concentric circles, then smudge them together.
c. Pour paint to create concentric circles, then print the onion round and round the circle until the centre is reached.

Display

1. Cover the background with purple paper and place the onion prints in vertical lines.
2. Cut out painted onion prints and overlap them in spaces around the display.
3. Choose three or four patterns and prints to cut out and suspend from the ceiling.

Winter vegetables are a beauty to behold because of their vibrant colours or strong ringed patterns. Onions reveal purples, blues, and circular patterns, while cabbages are many shades of green with undulating patterns.

Green Cabbages

Materials

Drawing paper
Drawing pencils
Ready-mixed
    paint (dark
    green, light
    green, blue,
    yellow, white)
Paintbrushes
Mixing palettes
Water pots

Method

1. Photocopy sliced cabbage leaves to create an interesting pattern.
2. Using the photocopy as a reference, carefully scale up the pattern onto drawing paper.

3. Observe the colours of the cabbage closely. Do the children notice that the vegetable is as close to yellow as it is to green?
4. Colour-mix shades of green and paint the cabbage, noticing patterns, textures and shading.
5. Fill the background with shades of green.

Display

1. Display the cabbage paintings blocked edge to edge, then add lime-green paper as a border to the display.
2. Twist green paper strips to spell the word 'cabbage'.
3. Cut up one of the paintings and staple the separate patterns around the display.

Christmas

Holly Paintings

Materials

White cartridge paper
Thin charcoal
Poster paint or acrylic paint (red, light green, dark green)
Gold powder paint, already mixed
Paintbrushes
Mixing palettes
Water pots

Method

1. Place a branch of holly on each table.
2. Using charcoal, draw holly leaves all over the paper.
3. Now carefully paint the leaves in two shades of green.
4. With the tip of the brush at right angles to the paper make red pointillist marks to represent the berries.
5. Once the page is almost full, fill the background with gold paint.

Display

1. Block together the holly paintings in vertical rows.
2. Separate the rows with strips of red and silver paper.
3. Cut out holly leaves from strips of red sugar paper and suspend the strips in front of the display.

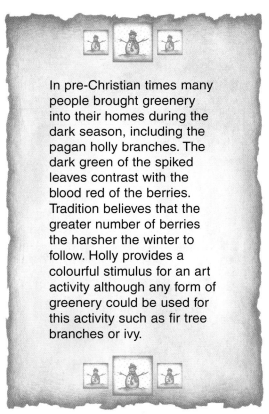

In pre-Christian times many people brought greenery into their homes during the dark season, including the pagan holly branches. The dark green of the spiked leaves contrast with the blood red of the berries. Tradition believes that the greater number of berries the harsher the winter to follow. Holly provides a colourful stimulus for an art activity although any form of greenery could be used for this activity such as fir tree branches or ivy.

Christmas Angels

Materials

Black paper
White poster paint

Method

1. Draw an angel in paint using shapes, namely triangles and circles on black paper.
2. Pour white poster paint straight from the bottle to form circles for the head and halo, triangles for the arms and inverted triangles for the wings.
3. Add poured paint patterns inside the angel shape.
4. Raise the paper, allowing the poured paint to run and form feathery lines.
5. When they are dry, it is possible to cut out shapes using a craft knife. Fill the shape from the back of the painting with white tissue paper, to create a transluscent effect.

3D Angels

Materials

Strong white card	Pencils	PVA glue	Wire cutters
Rulers	Scissors	Thin wire	Sellotape

Method

1. Cut out two triangles from white card.
2. Measure the centre of the base of the triangle and cut a slit at the top and bottom.
3. Now slide the two triangles together.
4. Draw and cut out a circle in white card. Find the centre and cut along the radius.
5. Slot into the body using glue if required.
6. Make a halo by drawing round a circle and cutting out the centre. Attach with thin wire to the back of the head, using sellotape.

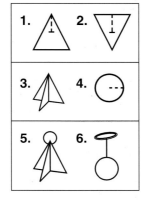

Display

1. Display the Christmas angel paintings in vertical lines on a pale background.
2. Hang some of the paintings on silver threads in front of the wall display.
3. Stand the 3D angels on the table top.

Clocks

The ticks of the clock take us from the old year to the New Year. All around the world the countdown begins just before midnight. Watches are often given as gifts. Clocks such as Big Ben strike twelve and the celebrations begin with the birth of the New Year.

Clock Montage

Materials

Black display paper	White chalk	Hessian fabric	Acrylic paint (white)
Craft paper (brown)	Black charcoal	Circular objects to draw around	PVA glue

Method

1. Create a display of clocks to demonstrate the patterns in the workings of a time-piece.
2. Draw around a circle on brown craft paper or hessian, then add cog-like patterns on the outside edge.
3. Cut out the cog pattern.
4. Continue to draw around different-sized circles on craft paper and hessian.
5. To make a collage, glue the cogs onto the black paper, to create an overlapping pattern.
6. Chalk cogs and wheels over, around and between the collage cogs.
7. Create additional chain and cog patterns by pouring white paint directly from the bottle onto the display.

Designer Watches

Materials

Paper	Black paint	Water pots
Drawing pencils	Paintbrushes	Ruler
Fluorescent paint (red, yellow, blue, pink, orange)	Mixing palettes	

Method

1. Create a designer watch. The face can be any shape, such as a face, flower, star or an abstract shape.
2. Use a ruler to draw the strap.
3. Add patterns and details to the drawing.
4. Carefully paint the watches using fluorescent paints and black paint.
5. When dry, cut the watches out and mount them on black paper. Cut around them, following the shape of the watch.

Display

1. Display the designer watches inside large wrist-watch shapes on the wall.
2. Make a large silver watchstrap and cut out circular purple faces.
3. Place all the individual designer watches on the face or watch strap.
4. Cut out cogs from cerise and purple paper, and overlap them on the display.
5. Cut the title 'Time Flies' from silver paper.
6. Finally, add a 3D display of clocks in front of the display.

Patterns of 28 and 29

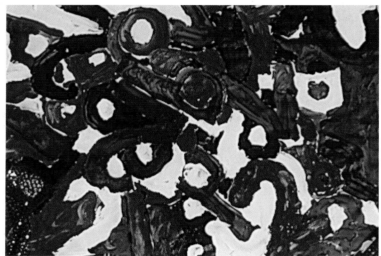

Number Pot-pourri

Materials

Cardboard stencils
  of numbers 2, 8, 9
Drawing paper
Drawing pencils

Acrylic paint (red, blue, black, white)
Paintbrushes
Mixing palettes
Water pots

February is an unusual month as it is the shortest month of the year and has 29 days every leap year. Each year runs over by one quarter of a day. Over four years another whole day is created, thus making it leap year.

Method

1. Investigate patterns of 28 and 29. Look at 4 x 7, 7 x 4, 14 x 2, 2 x 14. 29 is a prime number. What does that mean?
2. Randomly draw around the 2, 8 and 9 number stencils on white paper to create an interesting pattern.
3. Draw some as if they are in the background using broken lines.
4. When the paper is full, paint with red, blue, white and black acrylic paints. Try to keep the edges straight.
5. Fill in the background using the same colours but change the colours regularly so that you do not lose what has already been painted.

3D Numbers

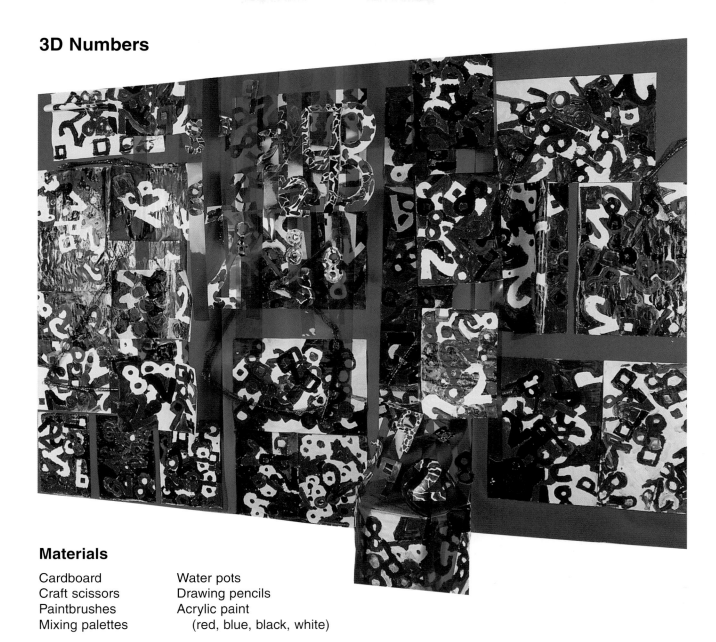

Materials

Cardboard
Craft scissors
Paintbrushes
Mixing palettes

Water pots
Drawing pencils
Acrylic paint
    (red, blue, black, white)

Method

1. Cut out cardboard numbers (2, 8 and 9).
2. Make the numbers different sizes by scaling them up or down.
3. Paint the cardboard numbers with designs in the same colours as the artwork. Try jigsaw patterns with white gaps between them, or stripes, dots and snaking roadways.

Display

1. Cover the background wall with blue paper.
2. Staple the paintings in formal lines, some edge to edge. Make different patterns as you move along the wall.
3. Suspend two or three paintings from the ceiling on strips of blue Cellophane.
4. Staple the large cardboard numbers to lengths of blue Cellophane and hang them from the ceiling in front of the display.
5. If possible, use a small display unit in front of the display and cascade the numbers on blue Cellophane from the walls and over the display unit to the floor, to form a waterfall of numbers.

Spring-cleaning

Spring brings lighter weather and traditionally is the time of the year to freshen up the house by giving it a thorough spring-clean (reaching into all the corners and cleaning underneath the furniture). Spring-cleaning is an unusual stimulus for art but it offers interesting opportunities to use cleaning implements, such as sweeping brushes, dusters, mops, polish, soap and dustpans, in unusual ways.

Cleaning Implements

Materials

Cleaning implements
   (brushes, mops, dustpans,
   polish, soaps, dusters)
Drawing paper
Thin charcoal

Acrylic paint (cerise,
   purple, yellow)
Paintbrushes
Mixing palettes
Water pots

Method

1. Draw the selection of cleaning implements in charcoal to fill the drawing paper.
2. Design a wallpaper pattern to fill the background behind the implements drawn.
3. Carefully paint it using acrylic paint in the colours cerise, purple and yellow only.
4. Display the work blocked closely together around a corner. Bend and ripple individual pieces to add a 3D element to the display.

Duster Painting

Materials

Drawing paper
Dusters
Acrylic paint (cerise,
   yellow, purple, cyan)

Method

1. Paint patterns with
   dusters by dipping
   them into the
   coloured paint.
2. Use different corners
   of the duster for
   different colours and
   remember to wash
   the dusters out.
3. Pour paint patterns
   over the top of the
   duster painting to
   mimic the patterns
   underneath.

Clean Sweep

Materials

Roll of paper 2.5 by 8 metres   Large containers to hold the paint
Household sweeping brush   Acrylic paint (cerise, yellow, purple, cyan blue)

Method

1. Place the sweeping brush in the paint, then sweep it over the rolled-out paper, to and fro.
2. Continue until the paper is filled.
3. There is no need to wash the brush between colours as it sweeps clean every time, and a natural colour-
   mixing occurs.

Display

1. Use the large brush painting as the backing paper for the display.
2. Display the duster paintings on the background paper and edge with light blue or turquoise edging roll.
3. Fill spaces by rouching individual paintings to create a rippled effect.

Bulbs and Growth

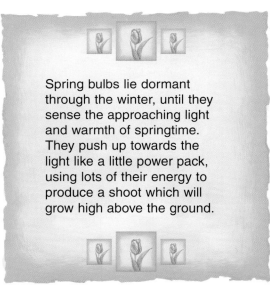

Spring bulbs lie dormant through the winter, until they sense the approaching light and warmth of springtime. They push up towards the light like a little power pack, using lots of their energy to produce a shoot which will grow high above the ground.

Pastel Bulbs

Materials

Bulbs   Black paper   Coloured pastels

Method

1. Closely observe and draw a bulb, scaling it up to twice the size.
2. Look more and more closely to find more detail to draw.
3. Overlay the pastels to gain different effects.

Bulb Collages

Materials

Bulbs   Tissue paper
Grey/stone paper   (black, brown, orange)
Drawing pencils   PVA glue

Method

1. Draw the shape of the bulb with pencil on grey/stone paper.
2. Glue the outer edge of the bulb with PVA glue.
3. Tightly twist strips of black, brown or orange tissue paper and glue around the edge of the bulb. Continue to do this, choosing a different colour each time and gluing it close to the last row.
4. Keep filling in until the centre is reached.

Painted Bulbs

Materials

Bulbs
Drawing paper
Drawing
  pencils
Ready-mixed
  paint
  (primary
  colours: red,
  yellow, blue)
Paintbrushes
Mixing
  palettes
Water pots

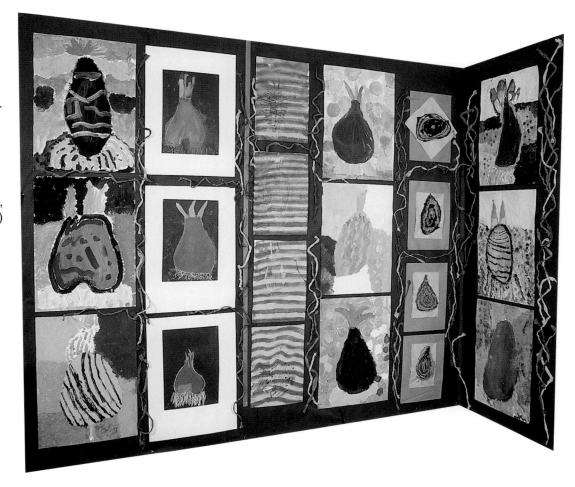

Method

1. Draw the bulb large enough to fill the paper.
2. Talk about growth patterns, look at the roots and shoots of bulbs and illustrate these.
3. Paint the bulb picture using ready-mix paints.
4. Fill the background with blocks of colour to create a pattern or skyline.

Wax Crayon Bulbs

Materials

Bulbs
Drawing paper
Wax crayons

Blue and green inks
Paintbrushes

Method

1. Draw a bulb in wax crayon, pressing hard.
2. Fill a paintbrush with ink and paint stripes across the page either vertically, horizontally or diagonally.
3. Change to a second colour of ink and continue to paint stripes down the page until the crayon shines through under the ink.

Display

1. Use black backing paper to display the work.
2. Display the work in vertical columns to illustrate the different techniques used.
3. Finally, twist three shades of green tissue paper to form shoots and roots between the work and attach from the top of the display to the base.

Blossom

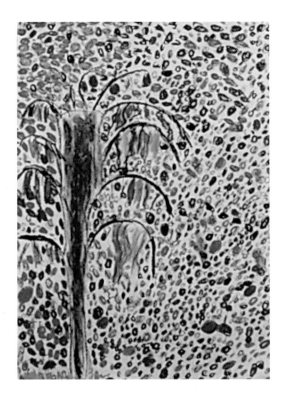

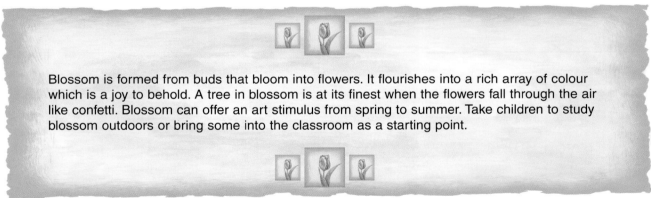

Blossom is formed from buds that bloom into flowers. It flourishes into a rich array of colour which is a joy to behold. A tree in blossom is at its finest when the flowers fall through the air like confetti. Blossom can offer an art stimulus from spring to summer. Take children to study blossom outdoors or bring some into the classroom as a starting point.

Blossom Paintings

Materials

Paper	Drawing pencils	Mixing palettes
Acrylic paint (white, red, blue, brown)	Paintbrushes	Water pots

Method

1. Paint a fine, delicate tree in brown paint.
2. Colour-mix many shades of pink and use them to paint lines of blossom in varying colours. Keep adding blossom tumbling down the branches in as many shades of pink and lilac as possible.
3. Fill the background behind the tree with painted petals as if they are being blown from the tree.

Variation

Try the same subject using oil pastels. Remember to smudge them to make new colours. Experiment with this medium until the picture is complete and all the background filled in.

3D Blossom

Materials

Tissue paper (white, shades of pink and pale blue)
String
PVA glue
Selection of small artificial flowers and leaves

Method

1. Talk about the way blossom tumbles down from the branches of a tree.
2. Cut lengths of string about 40 centimetres long and add lateral branches by tying them on.
3. Cut lengths of tissue paper and scrunch them up to make blossom.
4. Glue the string and attach the scrunched-up tissue. Remind the children to mix the colours.
5. Enhance by tying small artificial flowers and leaves to the hanging.

Display

1. Place pink backing paper on a display board.
2. Place four paintings to form a rectangle in the centre of the display. On either side, place two larger paintings.
3. Suspend paintings from the ceiling, attached to two parallel lines of paper.
4. Add twisted and fanned lengths of translucent paper and attach them to the ceiling. Fasten by stapling to a table top.
5. Cover the table top with pink paper or fabric and scatter with artificial flowers and 3D blossom. Trail lines of 3D blossom around the display.

Umbrellas

Les Parapluies

Materials

Drawing paper
Drawing pencils
Acrylic paint (primary colours:
   red, yellow, blue; white, black)

Paintbrushes
Mixing palettes
Water pots

Method

1. Discuss Renoir's painting, *Les Parapluies*.
2. Scale up the characters, placing them in any order to make their own version.
3. Paint the picture using acrylic paints.
4. Paint the background patterns and add the trees using the Impressionist style.

Display

1. Prepare blue backing paper to display the work.
2. Display the children's paintings of *Les Parapluies* blocked close together.
3. Drape lengths of blue Cellophane in front of the display to look like rain.
4. Hang umbrellas open or closed or place them on the floor around the display.
5. A print of Renoir's *Les Parapluies* can be displayed alongside the children's work.

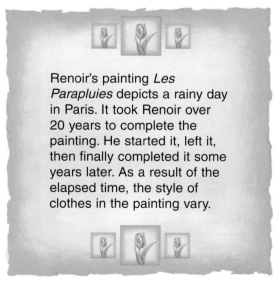

Renoir's painting *Les Parapluies* depicts a rainy day in Paris. It took Renoir over 20 years to complete the painting. He started it, left it, then finally completed it some years later. As a result of the elapsed time, the style of clothes in the painting vary.

3D Umbrellas

Materials

Drawing paper
Drawing pencils
Selection of blue paper
Acrylic paint (cyan, royal blue, white)
Blue Cellophane
PVA glue

Method

1. Cut umbrella shapes from different shades of blue paper.
2. Glue them onto the drawing paper to create a 3D collage effect.
3. Experiment with poured-paint patterns or strips of Cellophane to form rain over the umbrellas.
4. Encourage the children to flail the paint directly from the bottle to create thin lines that give the effect of a deluge.

Marbling Puddles

In spring the days start growing longer and warmer. When it rains, natural puddles form on pavements, roads and playgrounds. They are fun to splash in but also provide an outdoor art activity.

Ink Marbling

Materials

White cartridge paper   Marbling inks   Pipettes

Method

1. Use a pipette to drop two or three colours of marbling ink onto a puddle of water.
2. Carefully place the paper in the middle of the puddle, over the ink.
3. When the paper starts to curl, lift it off and leave it to dry.
4. Repeat using different combinations of colour to achieve different patterns.

Oil Pastel Marbling Pictures

Materials

Marbling picture   Oil pastels
White cartridge paper

Method

1. Study a marbling picture and decide on the colours needed to recreate the pattern using oil pastels.
2. Carefully draw the pattern and colour with the appropriate pastels.
3. Fill in the background, mimicking the patterns in the marbling picture.

Marbling Montage

Materials

Large sheets of card

Torn strips of cartridge paper

Trays filled with water

Marbling inks

PVA glue

Method

1. Pour drops of ink onto the trays of water (use two or three colours).
2. Dip a torn strip of paper into the inks.
3. Lift it off and leave it to dry. Repeat several times, using different combinations of colour.
4. Glue the strips on a large piece of card to create a montage of marbling. Continue to add strips until the card is full.

Display

1. Block the ink marbling and oil pastel pictures together side by side and edge to edge until the display board is full.

2. Hang more work in front of the wall display by attaching the paintings to parallel lines of paper roll and suspending from the ceiling.
3. Create ladders with the torn paper marbling, suspending them like rungs.
4. Use any remaining work to wrap around 3D objects, forming a pot garden in front of the display.

Mother's Day

Mother's Day or Mothering Sunday refers to the fourth Sunday in Lent when mothers traditionally receive presents and cards from their children. Use this tradition as an art stimulus to create some unusual cards and gift boxes.

Special Gift Boxes

Materials

Selection of small boxes
Silver hologram stars
Mixed stars and moons (multicoloured)
Gold, silver, copper, bronze paints

Paintbrushes
PVA glue
Chocolates

Method

1. Paint a small box with gold, silver, copper or bronze paints.
2. Paint the interior of the box and allow it to dry.
3. Glue stars and moons on the lid and main walls of the box. Add patterns around the rim of the lid.
4. Fill the box with a selection of bought or home-made chocolates for Mother's Day.

Mother's Day Cards

Materials

Gift boxes
Thin white card
Drawing pencils

Corrugated card, gold and silver
Glitter (choice of colours)

Mixed stars and moons (multicoloured)
PVA glue

Method

1. Draw around the lid of a gift box on corrugated gold or silver cardboard and cut it out. This can form the centrepiece of the greetings card.
2. Alternatively, draw around the lid on the white card and cut out the centre to form a picture frame. Stick the corrugated card on the inside.
3. Create patterns on the card using mixed stars and moons.
4. Highlight areas for glitter. Spread glue over them generously and pour on the glitter.
5. Add radiating patterns diagonally across the card using cut-out pieces of very thin corrugated gold or silver card, if desired.

Display

1. Small boxes are best displayed using mirror tiles to reflect the backs of the boxes.
2. Stand the cards alongside the appropriate boxes.
3. Run a twisted fabric between the cards and gift boxes to provide some continuity and flow through the display.

Grand Prix

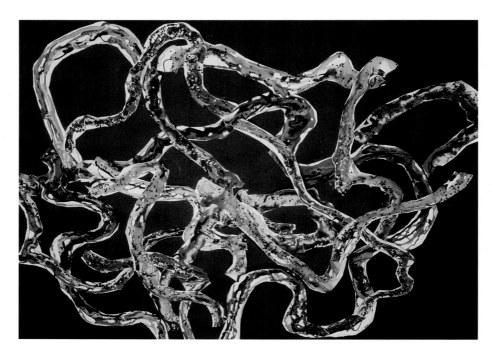

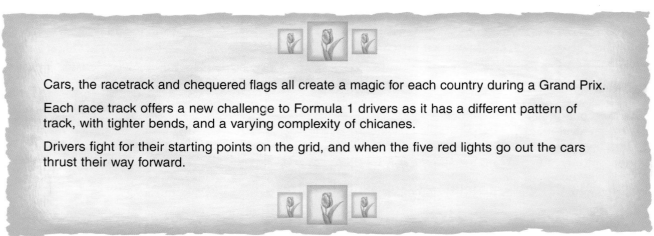

Cars, the racetrack and chequered flags all create a magic for each country during a Grand Prix.

Each race track offers a new challenge to Formula 1 drivers as it has a different pattern of track, with tighter bends, and a varying complexity of chicanes.

Drivers fight for their starting points on the grid, and when the five red lights go out the cars thrust their way forward.

Racetrack Art

Materials

White card
Drawing pencils
Acrylic paint (black)

Ready-mixed paint (red, blue, pink, yellow, green)
Glitter (range of colours)

Method

1. Design a racetrack for Formula 1 and draw using parallel lines.
2. Follow the track with black acrylic paint poured straight from the bottle.
3. Take different colours of bottled paint in turn and pour each paint to depict a racing car going around the track.
4. Remember that some cars do not finish the race, while others stop and start again and some go into spins. Can they show all these movements in poured paint?
5. Pour glitter onto the wet paint to represent the lights on the track.
6. Allow to dry until the paint has hardened, then cut out the tracks.

Designer Racing Cars

Materials

White cartridge paper
Thin card
Drawing pencils

Acrylic paint (blue, red,
    yellow, green, white, black)
Paintbrushes

Mixing palettes
Water pots

Method

1. Talk about racing cars. Use descriptive words such as 'sleek', 'low', 'aerodynamically designed' and 'bodyline'.
2. Make several sketches of racing cars and choose the best drawing to scale up on thin card.
3. Paint the cars, adding as much detail as possible.
4. Allow the cars to dry, then cut them out.

Display

1. Prepare a black background for the Grand Prix display.
2. Cut out the racetracks and their centres, and staple them in a random fashion onto the background. Keep some of them to hang in front of the display so that viewers can look through them.
3. Display the racing cars between the tracks and hang some from the ceiling at various heights.
4. Shiny tape can be taken through the art and stapled onto the wall as a finishing line.
5. Finally, assemble a 3D table top display of any Grand Prix memorabilia available.

Green Confluence

Green Confluence Paintings

Materials

White cartridge paper
Thin charcoal
Acrylic paint (cyan blue, dark blue, dark green, bright green, white)
Paintbrushes
Mixing palettes
Water pots

Method

1. Draw river interwoven shapes on the paper.
2. Add patterns to the shapes and also to the background.
3. Colour-mix many shades of green and blue to fill in the patterns. Try to colour-mix so carefully that you cannot see a change between colours.
4. Keep painting until the picture is complete and the paper filled.

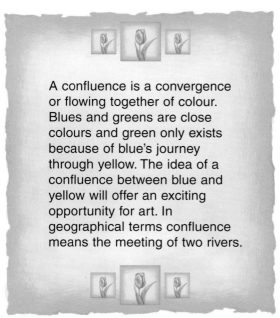

A confluence is a convergence or flowing together of colour. Blues and greens are close colours and green only exists because of blue's journey through yellow. The idea of a confluence between blue and yellow will offer an exciting opportunity for art. In geographical terms confluence means the meeting of two rivers.

Ripped Paper Confluence Collage

Materials

Large sheets of blue paper   Ripped lengths of paper (blues, greens)   PVA glue   Acrylic paints

Method

1. Glue ripped lengths of blue and green paper onto a blue paper background to create a confluence collage. Glue the edges so that the pieces stay flat.
2. Fill the paper with the ripped pieces.
3. Pour paint straight from the bottle, following the edges of the ripped paper.
4. In the same manner, add paint spirals to the paintings and leave to dry overnight.

Confluence Hangings

Materials

Long lengths of ripped paper   Pearlised paint   Mixing palettes
   (blues, greens)   (blue, green)   Water pots
Wooden bars or dowelling   Paintbrushes

Method

1. Staple ripped lengths of blue and green paper to a wooden bar or dowelling.
2. Mix the colours as the paper strips are added.
3. Paint patterns along some of the paper strips if desired.
4. Suspend the hangings against a blue or green background.

Display

1. This work is all in the same colour range so can be mixed together to vary the display.
2. Use sympathetic background colours (blue, turquoise and green).
3. Choose the work according to size and break it up with the paper hangings.
4. Whichever way you decide to arrange the work, the colours and diversity will provide a exciting display.

The Sea

Summer holidays often take us to the sea. The coast provides a wealth of shades, textures and movements to be explored.

A Colour Journey

Materials

White cartridge paper
Acrylic paint (cyan blue, dark blue, royal blue, white, yellow, red, black)
Paintbrushes
Mixing palettes
Water pots
Hessian fabric, tissue paper
PVA glue

Method

1. Take a colour journey through the sky, sea and land. Begin with wide brush strokes in blue to represent the sky.
2. Introduce blues, jade greens and aquamarines to depict the sea.
3. Continue the journey through the sand using wide strokes in various shades of burnt orange and ochre yellow. Think about the texture of sand and recreate using a pointillist technique.
4. Move into various shades of grey to depict pebbles and stones.
5. The last rows could be painted vertically with downward strokes to represent the growth of the earth and grass.
6. Enhance the painting with poured paint spirals and foam over the sea, undulating cloud patterns in the sky, or poured paint grasses and pebbles.
7. Finally, add tissue paper or pieces of hessian using collage techniques to create a 3D texture.

Variation

Create the same colour journey on long lengths of paper (3 metres by 45 centimetres wide). Display the paper strips on 3m lengths of wood. Staple the paintings onto the wood and suspend on hooks to form a vertical blind suspended from the ceiling.

Display

1. Prepare a blue paper background.
2. Arrange the paintings following a definite vertical or horizontal line.
3. Between the paintings, enhance the display with ripped paper pieces in a different shade of blue to represent the movement of the sea.
4. Add objects related to the sea, such as lobster pots, buckets, spades and fishing nets to create a 3D quality.

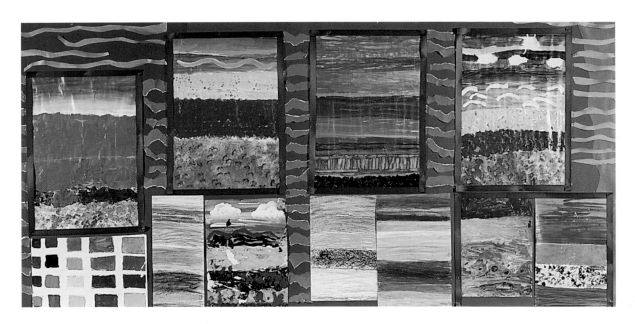

Shells

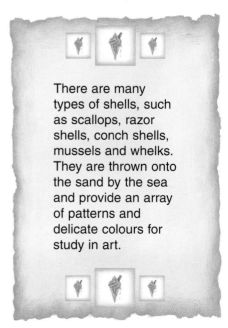

There are many types of shells, such as scallops, razor shells, conch shells, mussels and whelks. They are thrown onto the sand by the sea and provide an array of patterns and delicate colours for study in art.

Pearlised Shells

Materials

Large paper cut-outs of shells
Paintbrushes
Pearlised paints (red, blue, green, silver, gold, purple)

Note: Pearlised paints do not mix.

Method

1. Observe a variety of shells and study all the patterns and colours.
2. Cut out a shell shape and paint it in beautiful colours and patterns using pearlised paints.
3. Include as much detail as possible by referring to the original shells.
4. Add pointillist patterns to the shells using the tip of the paintbrush at right angles to the paper.
5. Display them close together to form a shell garden. Cut some shells up the centre and bend so they become 3D.

Tissue Oyster Shells

Materials

Large sheets of paper
Tissue paper (blue, green)
Pearlised paints (blue, purple,
    red, green, cerise, yellow,
    orange)
Paintbrushes
Glitter
PVA glue

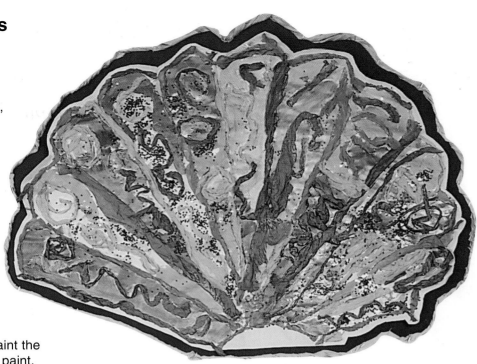

Method

1. Cut out a large-scale
   oyster shell from paper.
2. Paint lines of glue to
   create the pattern, then
   glue twisted tissue paper
   onto the shell for a collage
   effect.
3. When the collage is full, paint the
   background with pearlised paint.
4. Highlight areas with glitter, if desired.

Poured Paint Shells

Materials

Large sheets of black paper   Pearlised paint (red, blue, silver, gold, purple)

Method

1. Cut a large-scale
   shell shape from
   black paper.
2. Pour pearlised
   paint all over the
   shell to create
   patterns, using
   spirals, lines and
   zigzags.
3. Allow to dry
   before displaying.
   (See page 4.)

Display

1. Display the tissue
   oyster shells and
   poured paint
   shells on blue
   background
   paper.
2. Mimic the line
   patterns seen
   on the shells
   between shells
   displayed on
   the wall.

Silk and Sails

The summer season offers calmer seas and gentler breezes. Yachts can be seen sailing on the summer seas, with their beautiful sails of attractive colours and designs.

Sail Paintings

Materials

White cartridge paper
Drawing pencils
Pearlised paint (blue, yellow, red, white, black, green)
Acrylic paint (primary colours: red, blue, yellow)
Paintbrushes
Mixing palettes
Water pots
Glitter (range of colours)

Method

1. Fold paper to form a large triangular sail.
2. Talk about appropriate sail designs (for example, patterns in the sea, ocean colours, the sky).
3. Paint the designs using pearlised and acrylic paints in different areas of the sail.
4. Enhance the sails by pouring paint patterns straight from the bottle. Throw glitter in the paint to give shine to a chosen area.
5. Leave to dry overnight.

Silk Sails

Materials

Wooden dowelling
Silk
Gutta (silver)
Silk paint (shades of blue,
    green, yellow, red)
Paintbrushes
Water pots
Salt

Method

1. Make large triangular frames from wooden dowelling glued together.
2. Strengthen the frames by adding jinx triangles to the corners.
3. Staple the silk onto the triangular frames to create sails.
4. Draw patterns with silver gutta on the silk sails.
5. When the pattern is complete, paint with silk paints.
6. Add salt to create a different effect. This provides a pitted pattern if added to wet paint.

Display

1. Create a seascape effect on a blue paper background.
2. If possible, nail three pieces of wood across the ceiling about 60 centimetres apart in parallel lines.
3. Sink hooks into the wood to hang the silk sails.
4. Hang the silk sails from the hooks, varying their height. If available, use heavy knotted rope to give the feeling of yachts, boats and rigging.

Summer Sun

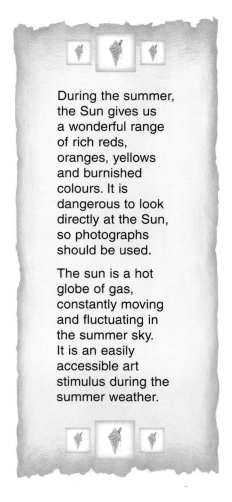

During the summer, the Sun gives us a wonderful range of rich reds, oranges, yellows and burnished colours. It is dangerous to look directly at the Sun, so photographs should be used.

The sun is a hot globe of gas, constantly moving and fluctuating in the summer sky. It is an easily accessible art stimulus during the summer weather.

Poured Paint Suns

Materials

White cartridge paper   Bottles of ready-mixed paint (red, orange, yellow, white)   Cardboard circles

Method

1. Pour paint in concentric circles from the centre to the outside edge of the paper to create a sun.
2. Use a cardboard circle and pour paint around it, if preferred.
3. Change the colours regularly to increase the pattern, and inlay one colour inside another.
4. Form flame patterns around the edge.

Painted Suns

Materials

White cartridge paper   Paintbrushes   Water pots
Acrylic paint (red, yellow, white)   Mixing palettes

Method

1. Paint pictures of the Sun from the core to the outside edge.
2. Mimic the gaseous materials and create flames around the outside edge.
3. Pour paint to form patterns on the surface of your sun if desired.

Fabric Paintings

Materials

Squares of hessian
Charcoal
Paint (orange, yellow, red)
Fabric medium to add to the paint
Paintbrushes
Mixing palettes
Water pots

Method

1. Draw the patterns of the Sun in charcoal on the hessian.
2. Paint it with the fabric paint.
3. Display the fabric paintings on two parallel lines of paper roll suspended from the ceiling.

Variations

a. Create collage suns by spiralling tissue paper to create a circle. Change shades and colours to reds, yellows, oranges and pinks to create individual patterns.
b. Draw pastel sun pictures on paper, starting from the centre of the page. Use oranges, reds, yellows and whites, to create the patterns.
c. Cut long flames from lengths of paper. Paint them and add patterns in fire colours. Hang them from the ceiling.

Display

1. Back display boards with a mixture of orange and red papers.
2. Display the work, mixing the collages and paintings. As far as possible, keep the vertical and horizontal lines straight.
3. In the spaces, place ripped orange papers to represent the rays of the Sun.
4. Hang the fabric paintings in front of the display.
5. Staple the flames to the ceiling so that they hang down and create a 3D fire effect. (See page 5.)

Ice Cream and Sundaes

The summer is a time to enjoy a cool ice cream or the decadence of a well-decorated sundae, with a chocolate flake and hundreds-and-thousands, plus a chocolate or raspberry topping. In a special dish they are a symbol of celebration and, with added decoration, they suggest fun and frivolity.

2D Ice-cream Paintings

Materials

White cartridge paper
Drawing pencils
Acrylic paint (red, yellow, blue, white)
Fluorescent paint (pink, yellow)
Paintbrushes
Mixing palettes
Water pots

Method

1. Take the taste buds on a journey through a beautiful ice cream using language and art.
2. Draw the cone and the balls of ice cream.
3. Paint the picture in acrylic paints using ice-cream colours.
4. Create a background, perhaps with shelves containing various bottles of ice-cream decorations.
5. Paint the background in bright vibrant colours and pour fluorescent paint over the background to make spirals, or to create the visual idea of a party.

3D Ice-cream Pictures

Materials

White cartridge paper
Coloured paper to form a cone or a fluted
  sundae dish
Acrylic paint (red, yellow, blue, white)
Tissue paper (various shades)
Foil to curl
Paintbrushes
Mixing palettes
Water pots
PVA glue

Method

1. Curl the coloured paper from its corner to
   form a cone shape.
2. Glue the cone to the background paper.
3. Cut the top of the cone with scissors to
   form an attractive edge.
4. Roll up coloured tissue paper to form the
   balls of ice cream.
5. Paint the background with ice-cream colours
   and add poured paint to give a juicy effect.
6. Add falling, twirling foil ribbons as desired,
   to create a celebratory feel.

Display

1. Cover the
   background with
   cerise paper.
2. Position the
   paintings and
   collages on the
   backing and edge
   with light blue or
   red edging roll.
3. Use some of the
   edging strips to
   form curls and
   attach them to the
   top edge of the
   paintings to give a
   party feel.

Gardens

Summer is the season when gardens come to life. Many flowers appear, trees are in leaf and the blue sky contrasts with the many tones and shades of colour in the garden. There are plenty of vibrant, visual stimuli during this season, providing an excellent opportunity for some outdoor art.

Sketchbook Garden Visit

Materials

Clipboards
Sketchbooks
Camera
Art packs containing:

drawing pencils	pastels
pencil sharpeners	oil pastels
erasers	paint
sticky tape	paintbrushes

Method

1. Visit a garden to see the dynamic shapes, colours and tones of flowers, trees and plants at first hand.
2. Organise the children into groups, each group having an adult leader with an art pack.
3. On arrival, tour the garden and select a favourite vantage point.
4. Collect as many sketchbook images as possible in order to recreate the garden from all the collated information.
5. Take photographs to help remind everyone of the view when they are back at school.

Gardens in Colour

Materials

White cartridge paper
Drawing pencils
Acrylic paint (red, blue, yellow, white, black)
Paintbrushes

Mixing palettes
Water pots
Personal sketches and collected photographs

Method

1. Compile the photographs and sketches from the garden visit.
2. Discuss the visit and ask:

   – What do you remember most?
   – Which is your favourite sketch?

3. Using drawing pencils, lightly draw the desired garden view until the visual information is complete.
4. Paint, using acrylic paints. Encourage colour mixing to obtain the right shades and tones.
5. Completely fill the background of the painting until the paper is not visible.

Display

1. Keep the display simple. The background paper needs to be a sympathetic colour to match the subject matter.
2. Position the paintings, placing similar styles together. If possible, line vertically with like sizes together.
3. Display a chosen picture in a frame and stand on an easel alongside the wall display.

Butterflies

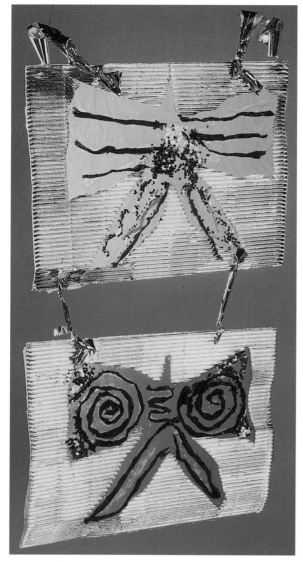

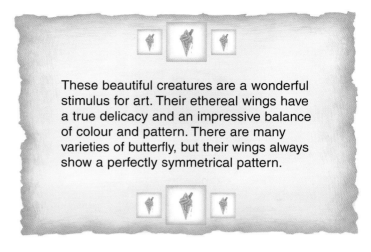

These beautiful creatures are a wonderful stimulus for art. Their ethereal wings have a true delicacy and an impressive balance of colour and pattern. There are many varieties of butterfly, but their wings always show a perfectly symmetrical pattern.

Poured Paint Butterflies

Materials

Rectangles of corrugated silver or gold card
Pearlised paint (pink, blue, purple, yellow)

Tissue paper
Sequins
PVA glue

Method

1. Pour the paint onto the corrugated card to form a butterfly.
2. Carefully cut out the butterfly, leaving the card rectangle intact.
3. Pour paint to form symmetrical patterns on the cut-out butterfly.
5. Use the left-over card as a background. Stick tissue paper on the reverse side to cover the hole. Twist tissue paper to decorate the butterfly and add sequins.

Camouflaged Butterflies

Materials

Thin card
Pearlised paint
Metallic paint (gold,
    silver, copper, brass)
Paintbrushes

Mixing palettes
Water pots
Tissue paper
PVA glue

Method

1. Fold a sheet of card in half.
2. Draw a butterfly with both wings matching. Use wavy lines, not straight.
3. Add painted lines and patterns, keeping them symmetrical on both wings.
4. When painting the patterns, start from the outside and work in to the centre of both wings.
5. Place crosses on any shapes they want to cut out.
6. Collage cut-out pieces from underneath with tissue paper.
7. Finally, pour paint on top of the wings to create patterns.

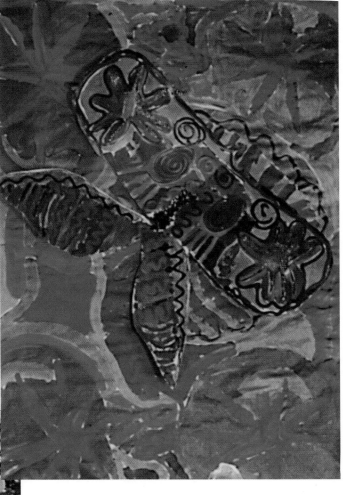

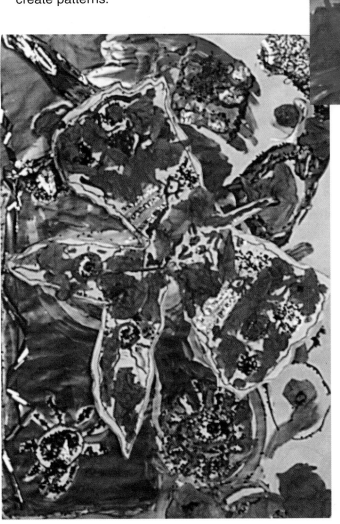

Butterfly Background

1. Look at the colours and patterns on your butterfly.
2. Create a suitable camouflaged design background for the butterfly.
3. Copy the patterns and colours of the butterfly onto the background paper so that the butterfly would disappear if placed on them.
4. Finally, pour paint straight from the bottle onto the background to match the patterns on the butterfly.

Display

1. Display the butterfly with the matching camouflage behind it. Attach it to the background so that it stands slightly away from it.
2. Edge the work with corrugated silver edging roll.
3. Twist silver paper or foil to form butterfly shapes and arrange in spaces around the work.
4. Enhance the display by spraying silver paint in spirals between the work (see photograph on page 1).

Summer Grasses

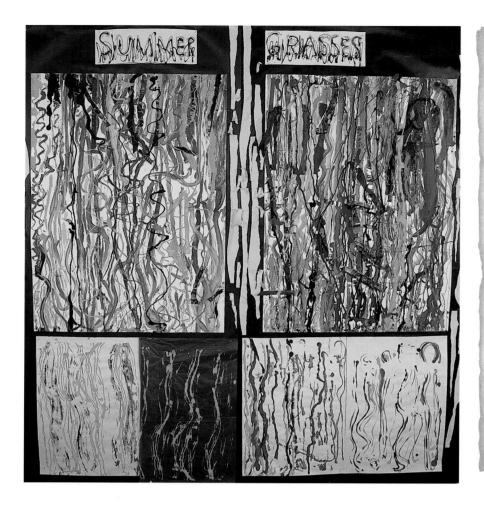

Summer offers many opportunities to gain first-hand experience of various grasses. Grass tends to grow quickly in summer and wonderful effects occur when the wind blows grass in different directions. It can become windswept and tangled and this image is a good starting point. Read the poem 'The Grass House' by Shirley Hughes.

Summer Grass Prints

Materials

Large sheets of white card
Large sheets of white paper
Tissue paper (mid-blue)
Ready-mixed paint (dark green, light green, yellow, white, blue)

Method

1. Outside, study the pattern of swaying grasses.
2. Pour lines of paint straight from the bottle onto card to form lines of grass.
3. Vary the colours and widths between the grasses.
4. When the card is full, place the paper gently on top of it to take the first print.
5. Now use another piece of paper for the second print.
6. On one of the wet prints, use the blue tissue paper to make another print.
7. Add more paint to the card and print again. Keep making prints until the paint runs out.

The Grass House
The grass house
Is my private place
Nobody can see me
In the grass house.
Feathery plumes meet over my head
Down here,
In the green there are:
Seeds
Pods
And tiny little flowers.
Only the cat
And some busy hurrying ants
Know where my green house is.

by Shirley Hughes

Grass Card Prints

Materials

Large sheets of white paper
Pieces of card
Rolls of string

Ready-mixed paint (light green, dark green, white, blue, yellow)
Rollers and trays
PVA glue

Method

1. Create a line of glue like a blade of grass from the top of the card to the bottom.
2. Add string and cut to the right length.
3. Keep adding different lengths of string until the card is full. All the string must be level in order to print.
   If children want to overlap grasses they will need to start a line, cut it and start it again on the other side.
4. Once dry, put paint on the roller and cover the string printing block, ready to print.
5. Roller the paint until the string is covered.
6. Place the printing block on the paper.
7. Roller a second colour onto the string and overprint the first one.
8. Continue printing until the paper is full of swaying summer grasses.

Display

1. Cover the background with shades of green in lengths down the wall. Add hessian.
2. Staple a variety of different work to it, matching sizes of paper and mixing prints.
3. Add the printing blocks too as this will show the process.
4. Finish with ripped lengths of green paper to form curling grasses.

Deckchairs and Towels

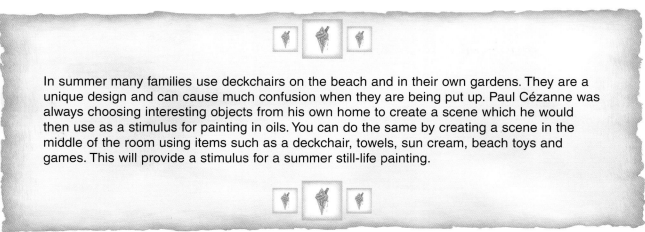

In summer many families use deckchairs on the beach and in their own gardens. They are a unique design and can cause much confusion when they are being put up. Paul Cézanne was always choosing interesting objects from his own home to create a scene which he would then use as a stimulus for painting in oils. You can do the same by creating a scene in the middle of the room using items such as a deckchair, towels, sun cream, beach toys and games. This will provide a stimulus for a summer still-life painting.

Still Life Deckchairs and Towels

Materials

Large white cartridge paper
Drawing pencils

Acrylic paint (red, blue, yellow, black, white)
Paintbrushes

Mixing palettes
Water pots

Method

1. Observe the still-life scene very closely. Ask:

   – What can you see?
   – What is the largest item?
   – What is the smallest item?
   – Which items are in the foreground?

2. Draw the items with light pencil marks to show the different areas of the painting, such as the foreground, background and so on. Draw confidently and try hard to represent them with an individual style.
3. Paint the work in acrylic paints, attempting to show light and shade through colour mixing.
4. Remember the importance of filling the background in completing the painting.

Charcoal Deckchair

Materials

Deckchair   White paper   Thin charcoal

Method

1. Draw the deckchair using charcoal on white paper.
2. What shapes can be seen in the deckchair? For example, can you see a triangle?
3. Draw the lines of the deckchair working from the triangle outwards. Add as much detail and shading as possible.

Fabric Designs

Materials

Hessian cut into rectangles   Paintbrushes
Charcoal   Mixing palettes
Ready-mixed paint (chosen colours, added to fabric medium)   Water pots

Method

1. Imagine working for a design company which has been asked to make new fabric designs for deckchairs.
2. Draw the fabric design for a deckchair in charcoal on hessian.
3. Paint the hessian using the paint and fabric medium in appropriate summer colours and designs.
4. Suspend the designs on rods and hang in front of the display.

Display

1. Cover the background with blue or black paper.
2. Place the charcoal drawings together in an interesting pattern.
3. Display the large still-life paintings to add a touch of colour.
4. Hang the fabric designs from the ceiling in front of the display.
5. Arrange the still-life scene on a table top in front of the display, along with appropriate objects such as shells, buckets, spades and other scenes of summer.

For details of further Belair publications,
please write to Libby Masters,
BELAIR PUBLICATIONS LIMITED,
Apex Business Centre,
Boscombe Road, Dunstable, LU5 4RL.

For sales and distribution in North America and South America,
INCENTIVE PUBLICATIONS,
3835 Cleghorn Avenue, Nashville, Tn 37215,
USA.

For sales and distribution in Australia,
EDUCATIONAL SUPPLIES PTY LTD,
8 Cross Street, Brookvale, NSW 2100,
Australia.

For sales and distribution (in other territories),
FOLENS PUBLISHERS,
Apex Business Centre,
Boscombe Road, Dunstable, LU5 4RL,
United Kingdom.
Email: folens@folens.com